THE TRUE SPIRIT OF AMERICA

Copyright © 2020 by Kevin E. Reaves

ISBN: 9798583081370

The True Spirit of America

Dedication

I would like to thank God my Father, the Son and the Holy Spirit for creating me in His image and giving me purpose. I thank Him for all the blessings, for building me up, for the gifts he has bestowed upon me, and for showing me more of Him so that I understand more of me. For that, I am grateful! To my wife, I thank you for your unconditional love! I am thankful for your support, your heart, your compassion, your words of encouragement, and for being the Good Thing that God has gifted me with. I love you, my queen. To my parents, I love you both with all my heart, and I thank you for the important lessons of life, and for helping me grow into the person I am today. Through it all you kept me focused on being the best I could be, and you kept me focused on God. To my Pastor, God has used you to pour into my life, and you have allowed me to grow within this great ministry! It is a pleasure to serve along with you to take True Gospel Christian Church beyond what we could ever imagine! Next Level Excellence! To all my family and friends, I thank you all for your influence in my life along this journey! You are so important to me, and I cherish our connection to each other.

These collection of thoughts, observations, conversations, and revelations of what God has shared and revealed to me, I share with you all! Over the past few years, I never thought I would share anything such as this, but I felt so compelled to write and reveal the things that I see taking place here in America. I wrote this in the hopes that all Christians, and anyone else who reads this, would have an open heart, mind, and ear, to receive this in the spirit. We all need healing from the things that have been going on from the beginning of America's existence to this present day! We have dealt with the symptoms far too long by covering them up with Band-Aids when in reality, we all need to face the truth that will begin the healing process. If you call yourself a child of God, then you are commanded by God to be a disciple, and it is our duty to serve God first, train and develop others, and send them out to draw more people to Christ Jesus. We cannot accomplish the complete works of God if we are always at odds with each other in earthly affairs. We will begin to look and act no differently than the world by causing absolutely no changes that the world can identify with in order for them to want to change. We are more than conquerors by the power of God, but we are being conquered by an enemy whose only power is the power we freely give it. We need to stand on God's Word and take back

what is rightfully ours as Christians and not stand aside divided by

worldly things. We should set ourselves apart from that of the world and

be great man and women of God! Hopefully, this collection of writings

will be as much of a blessing to you as it is to me. Thank you to the

readers.

Table of Contents

The Quandary of a Christian Black American

Foreword

Deacon Kevin is a loving husband to his beautiful wife, Chiyana, a respectful son, and a dedicated and faithful member of our church. Most importantly, he is a child of the living God and a true disciple of our Lord, Jesus Christ. Deacon, we are extremely proud of you.

It does not take great effort to discover that there are major issues in the land of present-day America. The greatest of all is evident in the myriad of issues that are dividing us. We are divided on religion, doctrinal beliefs within the same religion, race, politics, morality, and the basic concept of rights versus privileges. For years I have witnessed the decay and twisting of the truth which puts us in the cross-hairs of what the prophet Isaiah feared when he said, "Woe unto them that call good evil and evil good" (Isaiah 5:20). When I read the words of Deacon Kevin for the first time, I felt that I was reading the words of someone who had well-articulated his heart to God without judgment or leaning towards a political persuasion, but instead with a true heart-felt cry like the Psalmist David who cried, "Oh Lord, hear my cry!" (Psalm 61).

After reading the words of this manuscript I was immediately moved for several reasons. First, to see my spiritual son embark upon such an endeavor was indeed a proud moment. Secondly, I saw that his heart, his struggle, and his quandary were bleeding through. I saw a crying heart coming through in the words of someone whom I have known for many years and consider a friend. Lord, I will not support anyone who supports or stands for something that YOUR Word clearly speaks against. And yet, I still see issues that are not being addressed by either party. What am I to do? I am tired of voting for the lesser-of-two-evils at every level of government, whether it be national, state or local. Dr. Martin Luther King, Jr., along with countless others, stood for us to have the right to vote, but they did not stand for the obligation to vote against our convictions. Reading Deacon Kevin's words moved me to quickly see that perhaps many others would see and identify their own thoughts in the pages of this book but have been unable to organize them in such a fashion. Deacon Kevin has done that for you.

I must clear the air immediately. I am neither a Republican nor a Democrat. Deacon Kevin, like myself, is a principled voter. I consider myself a "Biblican" because I cast my vote based solely upon the Word of God. I determined as a young man in 1986 to vote based on my convictions and not my tradition. We in America live in a republic, which affords us to have representative government. Outside of God's governing order, there has been no equal. However, as great of a system in which we live, there are still major problems that have plagued us for years. Deacon Kevin addresses the quandary of these issues. More importantly, he offers the simple and revealing truth of how to resolve them.

It is with great honor that I write this foreword and speak in favor of this man of God. I encourage the holder of this book to take a few minutes to read this book, challenge yourself, and live according to the words Jesus repeated seven times in the Book of Revelations: "He that hath an ear, let him hear what the Spirit saith unto the churches."

Pastor Ral Waltower

True Gospel Christian Church

TrueGospelcc.com

Introduction

I believe in my heart of hearts that Christian Americans really need to hit the reset button. God is trying to open our eyes to what is most important in life, and we have turned away from standing on the solid foundation of His word. With so much political turmoil, racial injustice, and sin rising to authority, our focus has shifted! The Church is beginning to look like the world and the enemy is loving every minute of it. There is too much that we are allowing to happen in America, too many broken foundations, too much divide among churches, community, and race; and we are handing over the keys of authority to Satan. Instead of dealing with real solutions to our broken foundations, we treat the symptoms of America with Band-Aids. We need to begin to seek healing, and this healing is only achieved through our Father in whom we serve.

SYMPTOMS OF A BROKEN FOUNDATION

My Pastor once told a group of brothers that "if you only treat the symptoms of an issue, you will never get to the root foundation of the issue". A person who accidently cut themselves to the point of needing stitches will not resort to a Band-Aid from their medicine cabinet to stop the bleeding. You are just putting a small Band-Aid on a gaping wound! For many of us, when life is out of control and we are trying to stop the bleeding, we do everything we can to cover it up so that the truth is hidden from revealing to others who we really are. Every single person in this entire world must ask themselves the hard questions when dealing with a broken foundation of life in order to get to a real solution. You cannot ignore the truth no matter how hard you try to hide it! You can't just turn a blind eye to it, you can't cover it up with pretty clothes and makeup, you can't drink life away, you can't use drugs to escape from reality, and there is no sweeping it under the rug. **Band-Aid!**

The land of the Great United States of America—a place of equal opportunity, freedom, liberty, and justice for all! America the place where we celebrate our founding fathers, proclaim "In God We Trust" to build up this great land, and provide happiness of life. Painting a pretty picture of America is the American thing to do! We are the best of the best, and there is none greater than picture-perfect America. We barely have any dark blemishes, but even if we did, we just won't talk about those things! Instead, we can focus on the beauty of America and how great it is. We can idolize the flag, boast our patriotism, and take pride in our power house dominance of being a world superpower! Just sweep all that negative stuff under the rug and Say cheese for the camera! **Band-Aid!**

This is the tale of a one-sided story, a side that wants you to believe that this should be instilled in the hearts and mind of every person who is an American. But growing up as a black man in America, that picture is not always so pretty and clean. You grow up as young man thinking, *why do they hate me? What have I done to them? Why are my people being treated like this when we all are supposed to be proud to be an American? Am I not American in your eyes?*

As a young boy, I had awesome grandparents. They were very old school with little education, but they were so carefree, happy, and far removed from city life! They lived on a huge property where we had real family reunions, love, and happiness. As a young boy, I used to hear Big Momma and Big Daddy say all the time, "Colored People", without really paying attention to what that meant. To me, it was just how country folk talked in those days. Fast forward to around 1983 when I was in the 6th grade and enjoying life as a kid. Back then, a dollar to a kid was like gold, as we raced to the corner store across the street to buy candy—Tak's Corner Store! I'll never forget that there was a pool hall attached to Tak's, and it was always dark on the inside, although you could just make out the figures inside as they shot pool. I had always loved pool because my dad played, and he was really good at it, even won a few trophies. On this particular day was the first time I really paid any attention to the man sitting on the barstool just inside the door, and I noticed that there was a sign on the door that I had never really paid any attention to until that moment. I read it and it said, "No Coloreds Allowed".

I instantly thought back to my grandparents and realized that I was that colored person! I think back on that now, and it's amazing to me because the civil rights movement was in motion before I was even born, and yet my childhood in the 1980's was still dealing with the symptoms of a broken foundation! **Band-Aid!**

From freedom of the Mother Land to slave you learn about the struggles of your people, sold and stolen from their birth land. Footprints on this new soil, this new strange land, strange ghost like faces, some probably laying eyes on the white man for the first time, scared and bound by the chains on their neck, hands and feet. Not clearly understanding what they were saying when they were speaking with fast tongues, but knowing that it was about them, placed on auction blocks like cattle, and sold to the highest bidder. Wondering who America was really created for? **Band-Aid!**

BAD SPIRITS FROM THE BEGINNING

Ephesians 6:12 – For we wrestle not against flesh and blood, but against principalities, against powers, against rulers of the darkness of this world, against spiritual wickedness in high places.

Looking at the current state of America is not only embarrassing, but it is also a deceptive setup for demonic forces to run rampant seeking to kill, steal and destroy America. Demonic spirits have been unleashed, dividing this country more and more each day and we are blind to it all. Although America is one of the greatest places to live, the truth is that it holds many dark secrets that it tries to hide in its brokenness. As descendants of immigrants originally from foreign countries, we are here today deciding who deserves the right to be here and to have a chance at becoming an "American"! We erect walls and discard those that we do not like. "Go Back to where you came from!" I understand that we want to protect America from drugs, gangs, terrorists, and bad people. I get it, but who protected the original inhabitants of this land? And it's funny, because they want you to be proud to be an American, proud of this stolen land and its bloodshed of mass murder, that pushed the real Americans, the natives, to their doom. They called them "savages" in order to promote their own agenda and propaganda to get rid of a people who were just standing their ground against foreigners who invaded their home and their land.

They were reduced to reservations, and then they made a holiday of it and called it, "Thanksgiving".

History tells us of the great and wonderful Christopher Columbus, a man on a mission and journey to discover a new land, although the land he intended to find was not even America. I still chuckle when I hear statements such as, "When Columbus discovered America he found the Indians there." How can anyone discover a land that is already inhabited? And despite knowing that he did not discover America, we still dressed it up, made it pretty, we created again another holiday, and call it "Columbus Day". When they really landed on America soil, they colonized it, and built it on the backs of slavery. "In God We Trust" became a mockery and an insult to God the Father, God the Son, and God the Holy Spirit! I believe there are indeed Biblical influences woven into the foundation of America. Unfortunately, these influences have suffered grave abuse, misuse, and misinterpretation in the process of attempting to justify the enslavement of black people by using the word of God to distort the Truth. Over 400 years of this same old story being told to us and eventually, we found the missing pages they tried so hard to concealed from us, "Pharaoh Let My People Go", Exodus we broke free and God quickly began to reveal that their truth was not God's Truth and we became stronger in Christ Jesus! At last, we could finally get a piece of the American pie, right? Yes...No... Maybe? Or maybe we fought what we thought was a good fight and in return, only received half freedom. **Band-Aid!**

TRUE LIES TOLD IN AMERICAN HISTORY

It is the land of the free and the home of the brave, but sometimes it doesn't always feel so free. For some of us, we cannot be too brave, or we might fall victim to standing our ground. This story sounds familiar, as it is just like what they did to the Natives. Long after we built this land, raised the children of others, birthed children through rape and beatings; we were finally free and just trying to survive. Feeling unwelcomed as citizens and being mistreated in society, we struggled to overcome.

We fought with our voices, shouting "I AM A MAN!" The American History books flooding the school systems continued the lies with no intention of correction. Instead, they protect the "rich culture" of division that continues to divide all of God's children. History books reduce 400 years of history to only a couple of chapters about slavery, and quickly jump to a brief lesson in a short moment of our fallen heroes who fought for freedom and civil rights for people of color. Stolen invention after stolen invention, leaps and bounds of ideas of genius minds that were never given full credit. After all, we could not be viewed as being intelligent. We were not considered to be one of God's creations as only 3/5 of a person, right? Baboon, porch monkey, darkie, the infamous N Word. We were considered inferior to the minority, and they used violence and a barbaric spirit to keep the original man in their place, hidden from history, nooses around our necks hanging from trees. They recorded it in history with selfie photos standing next to their kill as if they were hunters with a prized buck! The Word of God says in Colossians 3:28, "There is neither Jew nor Greek, there is neither bond nor free, there is neither male nor female: for ye are all one in Christ Jesus." **Band-Aid!**

SWEEPING HISTORY UNDER THE RUG – THE CLEAN UP!

Now a thing of the past and a great point in American history, daily prayer in school used to signify unity between teachers and students as they came together as one. Sometimes, this was the only prayer a child would ever receive. What a great feeling that was. Eyes closed, no color, just people praying, "Our Father which art in Heaven, hollowed by thy name". After that, here comes America bearing its ugly head again. I pledge of allegiance to the flag", albeit a flag covered in a dark history against black people. With their hearts covered, children in school begin to feel a sense of false pride. Shortly after reciting the pledge they take the words of a man who wrote a song during battle, while dressed in his confederate banner flag, with a heart full of hate for people of color, and in true support of slavery now and forever. The passionate words he wrote about us as American people in the 3rd verse his song read,"

And where is that band who so vauntingly swore, That the havoc of war and the battle's confusion, A home and a country should leave us no more? Their blood has washed out their foul footsteps' pollution. No refuge could save the hireling and slave. From the terror of flight or the gloom of the grave!"

"Well… we can't use all these lyrics," America says, "and if we sing this verse especially, they will not fall for this. They've gotten a lot smarter over the years; I think we have taught them too much. Let's think… We'll disguise it, shorten it, put a veil over it, and title it "The National Anthem" **Band-Aid!**

BLACK AND WHITE – WHY DOES IT MATTER IF YOU SAY YOU BELONG TO GOD?

We have made great strides in race relations in America on both sides of the color line. Great relationships have developed, trying to move past our differences, moving towards a common goal of living in harmony and peace. This goal should be to love God as a body of believers, to enjoy the fruits of life, and to live the purpose that God has for each an everyone who is called by His name. You would think that after 400 years of slavery and up to the present, we would have gotten over all our differences in the color of our skin and understood that we are all God's children.

But there are some, like Pharaoh, whose hearts are still hardened by a past they took no part in. The remnant of this past of hate is still being taught and birthed through generations of an unbroken curse. Some will make an attempt to hide what they truly feel in their hearts about people of color with rhetoric like, "You should be grateful. Be happy; that was many years ago, and things aren't that bad like they use to be. Hey, I have black friends, I never owned slaves, and it wasn't me." As if those are words of encouragement to be said while choking the life out of you with their knee on your neck as you struggle to speak, "I can't breathe". No longer having to wear coward's clothing to cover their faces while riding in the night on their dark horses, they got better at the disguise. They traded that in for nice suits, corporate jobs, corporate power, corporate wealth, government positions, or even the good old boys in blue. The enemy smiles as he gathers his demonic forces to slowly infiltrate the destruction of America, and they devise a plan to continue the divide. **Band-Aid!**

PROPHECY TO MANIFESTATION "IF I WERE THE DEVIL"

How relevant it is today in 2020 that Paul Harvey's 1965 segment "If I were the devil" spoke so much detailed truth about America, giving us a warning of a somewhat prophetic sight into the direction America was heading. With these things coming to pass right before our eyes in a country strongly divided, the enemy is now penetrating the lives of people and causing them to become blinded by the political left, political right, democrat, and republican. Who's the lesser of two evils? Now Satan smiles with a huge grin at the thought of dividing and conquering a country simply by taking the true focus off God, driving it down a rabbit hole, and making people choose where they stand. Democrat or Republican? Which platform do you support?

So, who is on the right side and who is on the wrong side? I say both are to blame. Both have caused distractions, divided homes and families, broken friendships, racial inequality, and questioning churches that are doubting the Truth. All the while Satan is saying "Yes, yes, yes, yes! Let's keep this going. Give me the power to unleash my legion upon you all!" Satan sticks his foot in the door of America, sin becomes law, he steals the key and leave the door cracked just a little and says, "Let us sprinkle some racial unrest and a dash of pandemic. Yeah, I do believe this is working!" Satan says, "and now we got America right where we want them. Soooo God, they are not who you say they are...look at them, they are not even thinking about your Son, your word or you...they are nothing like Job...God are these the people you say loves

you, and love each other? They look distracted to me!" All Satan hears is

you talking not about God, but instead on who is right or wrong! **Band-**

Aid!

PARTY LINES DRAWN IN DECEPTION

Where do we draw the line between support and worship? I see

so many Christians debating about democrats and republicans that they

are beginning to look like the world. Did God's Word not warn us about

looking like the world bickering and fighting over being Red or being

Blue. But what about saying, "I'm a Christian, and I am not RED or

BLUE!"? Many are so set on the platform in which they believe in that it

is almost as though it is the gospel truth. They hold fast to its doctrine,

they do not sway from it, nor will they jump to the other side no matter

who the choices are as candidates. We willingly support a liar, cheat,

thief, dictator, deceiver, back biter, foul month individual who degrades

others, praises themselves, full of pride, has no humility, compassion, or

sympathy, and lacks accountability for their actions. But, it's all good!

After all, we support the platform and platform alone! Republicans and democrats compare platforms as if both are perfect in every way. We feel as though we must prove that our side is; better at keeping the fuel going, continuing the divide, and continuing the distraction as if God prefers one side over the other. **Band-Aid!**

Romans 2:11 – "For there is no respect of person with God".

A LIFE FOR A LIFE, IS NOT UP FOR DEBATE

Jeremiah 1:5—Before I formed thee in the belly I knew thee; and before thou camest forth out of the womb I sanctified thee, and I ordained thee a prophet unto the nations.

There were years upon years of injustice toward the innocent and century upon century of injustice toward people of color. Stored in darkness, they waited, until finally they were forced through a tiny door, single file line, into the bright light exiting the door of no return across the salty seas! Cramped in the bowels of ships, dying of diseases, jumping to the freedom of death, being bought and sold into slavery with many stripes on our backs, being bought and sold on the streets of the night, trafficking the young for an abomination of pleasure, babies dying at the hands of an abortion clinic disguised as Planned Parenthood, people of color hanging from trees with selfie photoshoots, by the hands of white supremist in a rage, a Klansman burning us at the stake, a neighborhood person playing police or a hunter relying on Stand Your Ground, to the bad, awful boys in blue, murder, murder, murder...kill, kill, kill... We debate over this as if one is greater than the other; as though one has more value than the other. We argue based in our passion and emotions; we argue until the cows come home! In the eyes of God everyone that is created in this world of sins is just as valuable to Him, including the baby not given a chance for life and the ordained thing. And so is the man or woman whose life was cut short without ever having the chance to fulfill their purpose of what could have been. And so is the person with a stolen childhood who grew up way too fast at the hands of a man or woman taking advantage of their bodies and creating years of pain and depression, essentially killing their soul for life. God is not pleased by any sin—a lying tongue, a deceitful soul, sexual immorality, murder, thievery. The list of what troubles him is long! While we are being influenced by the enemy of platforms, God says, "I Love you all. I love both the born and the unborn, and I desire them all to live and be treated the same! I sent my Son to show you the way. I gave you my only Son, the Lamb, the Truth of my Word, and this is what I get in return from those that are called by My name?" **Band-Aid!**

BIRTH OF THE POLITICAL CHRISTIAN – A DEDICATION TO MY FATHER-IN-LOVE

Recorded History (February 7th and March 19th) ignored! On March 25th, my Father-N-Love left a healthy strong "Hello…Alright" on our voice machine. No worries, we would call him back. It was our usual expected call to hear his voice right when we got home around 6pm at least every other day! And really, it was more like "Hellllllooooo…Allllright", in my Reverend Milton Thomas voice! On March 31st, 2020, when we were enjoying the day celebrating my Mom's birthday, we arrived home and checked our voicemail to hear the expected call from Dad. But this call was far different from the last call, and it turned out to be his last voicemail we would ever hear! At the time, we were thinking he had bronchitis as he had explained. In reality, he had been infected the whole time! We checked on him Wednesday,

Thursday, and Friday, pleading with him to go get checked. Finally, he gave in due to pain in his stomach. He arrived at the ER on Saturday, never to be released. There were up and down reports, we were all hopeful and in constant prayer, and everyone was fighting for him in the spirit. Siblings gathered together to show our love and to see his face, and he waited for all of us to hear our voices on that great day. The Father and His Son entered the room where he lay and welcomed him home on that Resurrection Sunday. There was a feeling of hurt, pain, and anger while we were trying to come to grips and make sense of it all, but we were happy to know that he is with God and in no more pain. However, a great since of righteous anger began to stir in me when I witnessed the political posturing of our elected officials as they argued, engaged in finger pointing, and turned the pandemic into a political game of dare. This offered no comfort to us. Our wonderful father and countless others deserved better, but unfortunately; we witnessed the rise of division.

As I stated in my opening remarks, Division and Separation are harming us at the core. If you have never had to witness a loved one suffering while struggling to breath, or never been unable to have a family member stand next to them to touch and pray over them, I say to the Political Christian: say nothing at all and be thankful that you have not experienced this horrible thing called COVID-19. I am ANGRY all over again, but I sin not! Instead, the Political Christians are so focused on electing or re-electing and proving their points and reasons with no true solutions in sight, while people are hurting with heavy hearts. Now, we are left with memories and voicemails just to hear his voice! **Band-Aid!**

VOTE – CHARACTER YES, CHARACTER NO

From the beginning God has shown us his character, and as His children, His little gods, we know very well what we should look like, talk like and act like because we have a Father who created us from birth. From the beginning, God has shown us His platform. For me, it is not character apart from platform, but rather character and platform that should not be unequally divided.

The devil's playground is keeping us all in bondage to his tricks, and we are providing the power and fuel to continue this mess we are creating in America. I can imagine Dr. Martin Luther King, Jr. in the presence of Jesus Christ and God the Father seeing the spirit of America.

Looking to the Son and the Father, he would say to them, "Forgive them; for they know not what they do". Somewhere down the line we have lost focus and muddied the legacy they set. My Pastor once said that people who are passionate about their party, only vote one way, and think their side has all the answers are truly misguided. Parties are man-made, and people vote on their own free will. It is your choice, not one that is controlled by God, but you and you alone. We should not reduce God to our level of politics thinking that God choose sides. God's choice will always be the totality of His Word, including His standard of conduct, character and his guide or platform in which we all should abide by. And don't get me wrong, God is always in control and He may allow things to happen, but we must make sure that we understand why they are happening! Is it for elevation or chastisement for bad behavior? Neither parties are perfect and if a lie is told in order to push an agenda or cover up the truth by deceiving the people, then they have committed a sin that God hates and considers an abomination!

God will not mingle with evil within any party line that gives partial truth to His Word. Both sides aim to benefit a certain selection of people, ideas, agendas and direction, all of which cause more division.

There is no true unity. This is the Art of War: keep the people divided. I hear far too many Christians say far too many times that we must take the "lesser-of-two-evils". Look at what the enemy has brought us to! Life and death is in the power of the tongue! **Band-Aid!**

A DIFFERENT VIEW BUT NOT SO DIFFERENT WITH YOUR SPIRITUAL EYES

My Pastor will tell anyone that when voting, you should always consider that you are a Christian first and should base your vote on your Christian values. Knowing this, voting becomes a tough decision because it drives us to question ourselves. Am I making the right decision? Some of us will run with that, and no matter who is running on the platform they choose, we are going to be ride or die like four flat tires. We back our candidate no matter what, defend the actions of their candidate, say that it's about the platform for which they are running on that confirms our vote, and will tell those opposing the candidate that they should not look at the character but focus on the platform. And then there are others that say they cannot get past the character of the person because they do not fit the platform they are running on. If you continue to listen to Pastor, he will tell you that if he doesn't believe the choices of candidates qualifies for that office of leadership, then it's a simple choice, and he will not vote for that office. BOOM!! Mind Blown!!

This is a very hard pill for some to swallow. After all, it is our civic duty to exercise our right to vote. Our people have died for this right, right? If we don't vote for the choices given, then we are giving a vote to the candidate on the other side—the dreaded enemy, the one who is going to destroy us all! If we get off the emotional roller coaster, begin to truly process what was said, and look at it in the spirit. We would see that we are no longer putting all of our trust in a candidate, platform, or even the office that is up for a vote. Like Pastor, we would be totally trusting and relying on God and God alone who covers and provides for all. This becomes a true faith walk by relying on God to work everything out for the good to those that love him.

Now don't take things out of context either. Pastor is not saying that we should not vote. After all, there are some people doing great things in our community, in our state, and in our nation that are sold out for God and not a platform. Here's a secret that my pastor tells us all the time (and this one is for free). Do you want to know what it is? Listen closely, and I will tell you. It is just a matter of doing the research. **Healing!**

SHOW ME LORD – AN ANALOGY OF CHOICE

What God has shown me as a Christian in this world when choosing a Pastor (The Candidate) and a Church home (The Platform) is that we set high standards and expectations of a Pastor to lead God's children in the right direction. We hold that Pastor accountable for their actions, and we expect that Pastor to have characteristics prescribed by the Word of God. You see that church headed in a direction that you want to be a part of and work within the ministry to help it grow to its greatest level. When the Pastor ministers the word of God, there is a stirring in the spirit that allows us to know that we are under true leadership. We can then rest and know we are being fed, all the while feeling complete joy with our decision and not having to second guess ourselves about the Pastor (The Candidate) and the direction of the church (The Platform). **Healing!**

ANALOGY OF CANDIDATE/PASTOR VS PLATFORM/CHURCH?

Should a Pastor lie frequently, cheat, disrespect the congregation and their spouse and children, or act any different from what we expect? We cannot and will not turn a blind eye to this behavior, and we will either address the issue, or we will begin to look for another Pastor (Candidate) that is leading a church (the Platform) that operates on the Truth of God's word and His principles. If we use and agree 100% with this analogy, how is it that we hold this type of standard to a Pastor leading God's people, but not hold leaders (Presidents, congress, commissioners, city council, etc.) to that same standard? Why do we look the other way when a candidate lies, deceives, and acts in bad behavior, but not the Pastor? We would not follow a Pastor doing those things, but we choose to follow a candidate who does? How is it that we totally ignore a candidate's or a leader's past and present and seem to easily forgive our candidate for all, but at the same time we point the finger at the other for their past and present, especially when we all have a past where a finger can be pointed right back at us? We all have made bad decisions, and we all have points of views that have since then changed with a new and better perspective. Woe is the Political

Christian that continues to drive the stake of division amongst one another. **Band-Aid!**

WHO CONTROLS THE CHESS PIECES?

We know that God is in control and that God allows things to happen in this world. Although we may get a few people to prophesy about a certain person, event or thing to come, it is within our own free will to vote and elect a man or woman to leadership. Sometimes that very same freewill and choice may not always be in alignment with God's will and plan for His people. He will allow it to happen to expose the ugly truth. This also means that every prophecy from someone who say they are a prophet may not be a prophecy of good news for the people. Sometimes I ask myself, what makes a prophet a prophet? Did God or man confirmed you as a prophet or are you a prophet that allowed your flesh to convert you to a fortune teller? But if you are truly a prophet from God delivering what thus said the Lord, then maybe sometimes what was spoken, could very well be a warning to the people that if we don't listen and turn our focus back to God for further instructions to lead us, then we will be no different than Sodom and Gomorrah! **Band-Aid!**

Matthew 7:21-23 – Not everyone that saith unto me, Lord, Lord, shall enter into the kingdom of heaven; but he that doeth the will of my Father which is in heaven. Many will say to me in that day, Lord, Lord, have we not prophesied in thy name? and in thy name have cast out devils? and in thy name done many wonderful works? And then will I profess unto them, I never knew you: depart from me, ye that work iniquity.

There is something terribly wrong with the way leaders are selected to lead in America. We have ignored these signs of division solely based on our party affiliations! The continued cycle keeps everyone thinking that if their party wins, it's a win for everyone. This is not true! In the end, nobody wins, and only the ones with worldly powers that control the candidates, the government, the direction, and their agenda are the winners—not you! In comparison, in the game of chess, some will argue that the Queen is the most powerful piece on the board. But it is not; it too is just a glorified pawn used to dominate the opponent, and sometimes the Queen is sacrificed at the hand of the Chess Master to force his idea to his own victory. Don't allow the hand of the Chess Master to use you by convincing you that you are a king or queen for the platform when in reality, you are just another pawn to defeat the opponent! **Band-Aid!**

THE CANDIDATES – THE HAVES AND THE HAVE NOT

Have you ever wondered why it is that to run for major offices in America, one must have deep pockets, million-dollar campaign ads, and constantly pimping—I mean trying to gain your vote! Their life is far different from that of the common man and they always give you the story of how they came up dirt poor, while poppa worked hard to gain the wealth that eventually put them in the position of wealth a life so much different from yours and for so long that they forgot what common life is about. Yet they run for office to make laws for us and create health plans that they wouldn't even dare use for themselves. But it's for you, because they truly and honestly care for you, right? Ok, maybe I am being too harsh, and maybe some do care. There are some with great intentions, but what makes a candidate change? Only the elite with qualifications fees in hand get to tell you "we the people"

what is best for you as they retreat to their gated estates!

WHAT WOULD GOD'S PARTY PLATFORM LOOK LIKE?

There is only one platform that every Christian should be

passionate about standing firm on, and it is not a democratic or

republican platform. Yes, we want to choose good leaders that can

effectively impact the lives of the people for the good and create

opportunities for all, but the continued fighting, debating, and

defending over these man-made platforms of false promises will only

help the enemy destroy this country. Yes, it is true that who you vote in

office may make good on some of the things you support about your

platform, but no matter what, they will never fulfill the entire platform.

We have yet to elect a president or leader, democrat or republican, that

has done everything they claimed to be in support of. Nothing you can

point out in either platform since you have been voting has not ended

the sin and injustice, nor has it given everyone a fair and true

opportunity at the dream of the American pie! The pie remains

unreachable for many, and for the ones who have it, ones in power will do anything to keep it unreachable! Evil has come from within both

parties because in the end, some candidates must make good on the

worldly agenda of the earthly power that supports them. **Band-Aid!**

But God being the awesome God with His perfectly orchestrated

mastery of the Holy Bible, sets the platform for the foundation of

healing. He brings forth everything we need to recognize the type of

leaders we seek, as well as what is required to use as a guideline in

choosing a leader. At the same time, it is also a measuring tool for every

leader to be held accountable to in their speech to the people, their

actions, their agenda, their intent in their heart, and their

characteristics. **Healing!**

God provides so many answers to this question that I can't list

them all, but even looking at a few of them will drastically open our eyes

to what a candidate should look like. We know that God is a great

component in the character of a person, and they must uphold Biblical

doctrine (platform of God) as described in the qualifications to be an

Apostle, Pastor, Minister, Evangelist, Elder, Deacon, a man of valor, a

proverbs woman, a child, and all others. Anyone who desires to lead others in office should be held to the candle stick and examined as a person that has all people in mind. First and foremost, they must display the love of God in their heart. **Healing!**

Before we vote for a candidate, we must first consider these verses:

- *1 John 4:1-5 – Beloved, believe not every spirit, but try the spirits whether they are of God: because many false prophets are gone out into the world. Hereby know ye the Spirit of God: Every spirit that confesseth that Jesus Christ is come in the flesh is of God: And every spirit that confesseth not that Jesus Christ is come in the flesh is not of God: and this is that spirit of antichrist, whereof ye have heard that it should come; and even now already is it in the world. Ye are of God, little children, and have overcome them: because greater is he that is in you, than he that is in the world. They are of the world: therefore speak they of the world, and the world heareth them.*

- *Matthew 7:21-23 – Not everyone that saith unto me, Lord, Lord, shall enter into the kingdom of heaven; but he that doeth the will of my Father which is in heaven. Many will say to me in that day, Lord, Lord, have we not prophesied in thy name? and in thy name have cast out devils? and in thy name done many wonderful works. And then will I profess unto them, I never knew you: depart from me, ye that work iniquity.*

Additionally, candidates must display the characteristics highlighted in the following verses:

- *John 14:15 – If ye love me, keep my commandments.*

- *Mark 19:14 – But Jesus said, Suffer little children, and forbid them not, to come unto me: for of such is the kingdom of heaven.*

- *Galatians 5:22 – But the fruit of the Spirit is love, joy, peace, longsuffering, gentleness, goodness, faith, meekness, temperance: against such there is no law.*

- *Philippians 2:4 – Look not every man on his own things, but every man also on the things of others.*

- *Exodus 1:17,20 – But the midwives feared God, and did not as the king of Egypt commanded them, but saved the men children alive. Therefore God dealt well with the midwives: and the people multiplied, and waxed very mighty.*

- *I John 3:17 – But whoso hath this world's good, and seeth his brother have need, and shutteth up his bowels [of compassion] from him, how dwelleth the love of God in him?*

A WARNING TO A CANDIDATE'S CAMPAIGN/PLATFORM – DO NOT BE CAUGHT DOING THESE THINGS

- *Proverbs 6:16 – These six things doth the Lord hate: yea, seven are an abomination unto him: A proud look, a lying tongue, and hands that shed innocent blood, An heart that deviseth wicked imaginations, feet that be swift in running to mischief, A false witness that speaketh lies, and he that soweth discord among brethren.*

- *Isaiah 5:20 – Woe unto them that call evil good, and good evil; that put darkness for light, and light for darkness; that put bitter for sweet, and sweet for bitter!*

- *Jeremiah 44:4 – Howbeit I sent unto you all my servants the prophets, rising early and sending them, saying, Oh, do not this abominable thing that I hate.*

- *Revelation 2:6 – But this thou hast, that thou hatest the deeds of the Nicolaitans, which I also hate.*

- *Romans 16:17-18 – Now I beseech you, brethren, mark them which cause divisions and offences contrary to the doctrine which ye have learned; and avoid them.*

- *James 4:11 – Speak not evil one of another, brethren. He that speaketh evil of [his] brother, and judgeth his brother, speaketh evil of the law, and judgeth the law: but if thou judge the law, thou art not a doer of the law, but a judge.*

- *Jeremiah 8:12 – Were they ashamed when they had committed abomination? nay, they were not at all ashamed, neither could they blush: therefore shall they fall among them that fall: in the time of their visitation they shall be cast down, saith the LORD.*

- *Proverbs 6:19 – A false witness [that] speaketh lies, and he that soweth discord among brethren.*

- *Matthew 18:6 – But whoso shall offend one of these little ones which believe in me, it were better for him that a millstone were hanged about his neck, and that he were drowned in the depth of the sea.*

- *1 Peter 2:1 – Wherefore laying aside all malice, and all guile, and hypocrisies, and envies, and all evil speakings,*

- *Leviticus 20:13 – Thou shalt not lie with mankind, as with womankind: it is abomination.*

- *Ephesian 4:29 – Let no corrupt communication proceed out of your mouth, but that which is good to the use of edifying, that it may minister grace unto the hearers.*

- *Romans 1:26-32 – For this cause God gave them up unto vile affections: for even their women did change the natural use into that which is against nature. And likewise also the men, leaving the natural use of the woman, burned in their lust one toward another; men with men working that which is unseemly, and receiving in themselves that recompence of their error which was meet. And even as they did not like to retain God in their knowledge, God gave them over to a reprobate mind, to do those things which are not convenient; Being filled with all unrighteousness, fornication, wickedness, covetousness, maliciousness; full of envy, murder, debate, deceit, malignity; whisperers, V30 Backbiters, haters of God, despiteful, proud, boasters, inventors of evil things, disobedient to parents, Without understanding, covenant breakers, without natural affection, implacable, unmerciful: Who knowing the judgment of God, that they which commit such things are*

*worthy of death, not only do the same, but have pleasure in
them that do them.*

- *Proverbs 11:2 – When pride comes, then comes disgrace, but
with the humble is wisdom*

- *Deuteronomy 12:31 – Thou shalt not do so unto the LORD thy
God: for every abomination to the LORD, which he hateth, have
they done unto their gods; for even their sons and their
daughters they have burnt in the fire to their gods.*

- *Proverbs 16:18 – Pride goes before destruction, and a haughty
spirit before a fall.*

- *Proverbs 28:9 – He that turneth away his ear from hearing the
law, even his prayer shall be abomination.*

- *Proverbs 8:13 – The fear of the Lord is hatred of evil. Pride and
arrogance and the way of evil and perverted speech I hate.*

- ***Proverbs 15:9 – The way of the wicked is an abomination unto the LORD: but he loveth him that followeth after righteousness.***

  Proverbs 16:5 – Everyone who is arrogant in heart is an abomination to the Lord; be assured, he will not go unpunished.

Imagine that when we entered the booth to vote, there were no 'R's' or 'D's' that preceded or followed a candidate's name. We would be more apt to abandon the party line voting and truly vote in a manner consistent with our beliefs. It would force us to do our research and homework. And as I mentioned earlier, this is an important charge from my pastor.

A LETTER TO THE CHURCH

Grace be unto you, and peace from God our Father, and from the Lord Jesus Christ. I thank my God always on your behalf, for the grace of God which is you by Jesus Christ. That in everything you are enriched by him, in all utterance and in all knowledge. Even as the testimony of Christ was confirmed in you, so that you come behind in no gift, waiting for the coming of our Lord Jesus Christ. Who shall also confirm you unto the end, that you may be blameless in the day of our Lord

Jesus Christ. God is faithful, by whom you were called unto the

fellowship of his Son Jesus Christ. Now I beseech you, brothers and

sisters, by the name of our Lord Jesus Christ, that you all speak the

same thing, and that there be no divisions among you but that you be

perfectly joined together in the same mind and in the same judgement.

~ Apostle Paul 1 Corinthians 1:3-10

As the Church, we must get back to the basics and focus on the things of God. God has nothing to do with the politics or debates of man, and God is neither Democrat nor Republican. He does not side with either party, and He is not going to side with evil vs evil. As Christians, we are immigrants from a Greater Kingdom, and we must live in this world and make the best of life. We must abide by the earthly laws, rules, and authority over us, but we must not forget the laws, rules, and authority of God our Father. Yes, as Christians we have the right to exercise our voice for things that are important to us by selecting leadership that is God-qualified by the standards God prescribes in His word and His word alone. I know you feel that your passion for what you believe in is the right thing, and it is evident in your reasoning with others as you state your case. But sometimes you can speak so loudly that you become muted by the people you are trying to convince. And sometimes, even unto God.

1 Corinthians 13:1 – Though I speak with the tongues of men and of angels, and have not charity, I am become as sounding brass, or a tinkling cymbal.

One thing is for sure, as Christians on both sides of the political lines, I know that we all have a common thread that sews us together; a thread that is trying to show us that if we use the power that God has given to us, we can combine those ideas that are right, just, and true to show the world what God can do through vessels of godly leadership. We could have confidence in knowing that whomever we support and vote for, we wouldn't have to cringe each time they said or did something, and we wouldn't have to quickly defend their actions in order to justify our continued support. In todays' society, because the lines are so blurred, we must be very careful of whom we support for leadership. We make a lot of excuses today to make sure our candidate fits the description and the platform that agrees with our agenda! This is my take on this: does the candidate fit God's description, God's platform, and God's agenda? If so, that is the candidate I want to vote for.

Galatians 6:1-18 – Brethren, if a man be overtaken in a fault, ye which are spiritual, restore such an one in the spirit of meekness; considering thyself, lest thou also be tempted. Bear ye one another's burdens, and so fulfil the law of Christ. For if a man think himself to be something, when he is nothing, he deceiveth himself. But let every man prove his own work, and then shall he have rejoicing in himself alone, and not in another. For every man shall bear his own burden. Let him that is taught in the word communicate unto him that teacheth in all good things. Be not deceived; God is not mocked: for whatsoever a man soweth, that shall he also reap. For he that soweth to his flesh shall of the flesh reap corruption; but he that soweth to the Spirit shall of the Spirit reap life everlasting. And let us not be weary in well doing: for in due season we shall reap, if we faint not. As we have therefore opportunity, let us do good unto all men, especially unto them who are of the household of faith. Ye see how large a letter I have written unto you with mine own hand. As many as desire to make a fair shew in the flesh, they constrain you to be circumcised; only lest they should suffer persecution for the cross of Christ. For neither they themselves who are circumcised keep the law; but desire to have you circumcised, that they may glory in your flesh. But God forbid that I should glory, save in the cross of our Lord Jesus Christ, by whom the world is crucified unto me, and I unto the world. For in Christ Jesus neither circumcision availeth any thing, nor uncircumcision, but a new creature. And as many as walk according to this rule, peace be on them, and mercy, and upon the Israel of God. From henceforth let no man trouble me: for I bear in my body the marks of the Lord Jesus. Brethren, the grace of our Lord Jesus Christ be with your spirit. Amen.

Beware of those that speak of these worldly candidates who have not been vetted against the word of God, or even measure up to the true qualifications that God commands for leaders.

1 Corinthians 13:2-6 – And though I have the gift of prophecy, and understand all mysteries, and all knowledge; and though I have all faith, so that I could remove mountains, and have not charity, I am nothing. And though I bestow all my goods to feed the poor, and though I give my body to be burned, and have not charity, it profiteth me nothing. Charity suffereth long, and is kind; charity envieth not; charity vaunteth not itself, is not puffed up, Doth not behave itself unseemly, seeketh not her own, is not easily provoked, thinketh no evil; Rejoiceth not in iniquity, but rejoiceth in the truth;

By having an open dialogue with all Christians from both sides and with all God's children of many races, I guarantee that we could develop a common ground to find out what is important and what we can all agree on. In the eyes of many Christians, black lives Do Matter. That's not to say that other lives don't matter or to discredit others, but we are in a time where things are happening to black people, black men especially, at an alarming rate that has many people, including myself concerned. At the very same time, all lives are extremely important to God—even the precious lives taken before entering this world. The child forced to sell their body and the countless number of people who never got to say goodbye to their loved ones due to the COVID virus are all important. None of them have priority over the other! We can all agree that we need great healthcare for everyone, support to our veterans and their mental health, reward our law enforcement officers who are doing the right thing and holding bad behavior accountable in an unbiased court of law! Creating great education systems for every single child in America, emphasizing equal justice and equality, prioritizing fair treatment for the young and old, and giving every American the tools needed to be successful citizens are the issues we should focus on.

Let's begin to examine those things that are not of God that are happening in America and taking us to a place of corruption, destruction, sin, and the continuing downfall of America. There are drugs, sexual immorality, the deconstruction of the family order, lack of control over the curriculum being taught to our children, and the acceptance of sin to becoming law. We want to freely serve and worship God, be free from discrimination for our beliefs, and not be forced to be silent like we have been for years. So silent that we look no different than the world. As my Pastor would say, Christians have become so silent against the wall that we look like wallpaper! There are plenty of things that we can come together and fight for to bring God's divine order to how America operates. Honestly, I say let's start a new party: a party that rests totally on the Word of God and produces candidates based on the Word. We must not continue being distracted by the things of this world that we are journeying through. **Healing!**

ELECTION DAY - CLOSING CHAPTER OF THOUGHTS

As a black man in America, I have always been observant of people, events in history, and the climate of America in different time periods. My perspective may not be your perspective, but it is what God has shown me through my lens. As I said earlier, America is one of the greatest places to live, but at the same time, I cannot help what I feel about America and the direction that it's going in.

From the beginning of its history, America has never dealt with the broken foundation of its existence. We speak of Social Distancing as if it is a new thing when all along it has been here since the beginning. We have been social distancing from the Truth of God's word. From the murdering of the natives to the present-day turmoil between the left and the right, ignoring the pain that American is in right now. We are just putting a Band-Aid on a gaping wound! One side must be right, and the other side must be wrong. There are too many agendas, too many different spirits in these agendas, and too many legions upon legions of spirits being unleashed on America. Many of our eyes are either closed or just refusing to see what is happening as long as it's not at our doorsteps.

Sometimes as a whole, I wonder if we were ever truly built on "In God We Trust" or if that is just a cliché we adopted to go along with our Red, White and Blue. I am a black man trying to love America, but America seems not to love me back when I see with my own eyes the injustice to people of color. My faith is strong and rooted in my Father, but as a black man, you can't deny that even as innocent as you are in your car doing 5 miles below the speed limit and obeying all the traffic laws, when flashing blue and red lights appear behind you, your heart beats a little faster, and thoughts of the last encounter in America race through your mind. And when they fly pass you headed to a call, you realize you are not the target today, there is a sigh of relief and then you begin to relax.

My growth in Yeshua my Lord and Savior has developed me into who I am today. My eyes and ears are wide open to see and hear, to be educated on the things of God, and to understand the things that are happening in the spirit and in the natural. I know that God is in control; it's just that the free will within us that keeps us distracted from God's control that has America waring against each other. We have got to get back to the basics of remembering that God is our focus and the answer to every problem, issue, and solution that America has. We have allowed the enemy to deceive us by settling for bad leadership just to address the things that are near and dear to our hearts. If "We the People" is a true statement, then why can't We the People come together on one accord as God wants us to be? Churches are divided, people are divided, America is divided; it's the great fall of a nation when division is the answer to everything.

How great it would be if the church would get back to the truth of God's Word as it is written and not misinterpreted to fit our life style or our own doctrine. My pastor teaches us that there is a difference between reading the Word of God and studying the Word of God. If you are reading it, you will only get information and inspiration, but if you are studying the Word of God, you will obtain revelation of His Word, revelation of Gods Truth, revelation about what's happening in America and this world, and revelations about who you really are in Christ Jesus.

How great it would be if the church began to train, develop, and send out Presidents, Vice Presidents, Congressmen, and all elected officials that are deeply rooted in God, not affiliated with any party line. Instead, they wave the banner of Christ as their party affiliation and the Holy Bible as their platform on which they run for an office. How great America would be to have confidence in our leaders knowing that they are not controlled by earthly worldly power, but instead totally dependent on the Power of God! That is when America will truly be great!

Will we as Christians continue to support politicians that lie and deceive America over and over? Even when they are caught on video, taped recordings, and quoted in interviews, they choose to lie to the people and tell more lies to support the lie they told! And in the same breath, they look across the aisle and point out lies of their opponents. Where is the image of God in that? How as a Christian do you justify that, based on the Word of God?

When God told his people to go and possess the land, they allowed the enemy to put fear in their hearts and divide the people in a decision that cost them 40 years in the wilderness. You would think that it took 40 years because they had a long way to go, but if you study the Word it was only about an 11-day journey to what God had promised them! Deferred Promises! How long will America defer the promise that God has for us? We do not have to vote for or promote foolishness, broken promises, or things that bear no fruit. If we don't begin to truly hold leaders accountable and become a voice as the true church of Gods people, then we will continue to be just like the people saying, "give us a king like the other nations"!

I know that we created this mess that we are in and that it will take time to fix, but we must not allow ourselves to continually be in the wilderness, develop a wilderness mentality, create wilderness generations, settle for wilderness leadership, or live a wilderness life. We cannot be fooled by every little thing we hear, see, or receive. We must research the truth and measurement of it by the Word. Stop relying on the media, social media, google, pimps—I mean politicians, or someone-told-me-that-someone-told-them information. These things have been heavily researched by those in power to steer the direction in which they want you to think and act in order to have total control over your life. Although American history is tarnished with lies and its teachings of history, it is with the unraveling of the truth that America will begin to heal. Yes, it will hurt to relive the truth for many, but it is within that truth that the greatness of what America could begin to right the wrongs and make things right. We must truly honor the history of the original people of this land, and we must truly highlight the rich history of contributions and great achievements that people of color broke their backs for just to be viewed as equals in society.

When we come together as a multitude of Christian people of all colors, we can stand our ground to eradicate the demonic forces and spirits of violence, hatred, division, lies, deceit, poverty and greed! Darkness cannot overcome light and must submit itself to it. As Christians, we are the light of the world and the salt that provides the flavor God adores! Wherever God's light falls, the enemy has nowhere to hide, exposed to the Truth, and must flee! We must take a survey on our thoughts and emotions and ask ourselves: if someone were to go to my social media page or get a glimpse of what was important to me on a scale, where would that weight be at its heaviest? Would they see more of God, love, family, friends, laughter, and fun? Or would they see a mixture of those things along with things of the world, such as arguing,

debating, division, and proving your point to support your views? It is

time for us to push reset and refocus our thoughts on those things that

are true, honest, just, pure, lovely, and of good report. If there be any

virtue, and if there be any praise, we should think on these things.

Healing!